The
DEVIL'S
FOOLS

poetry by

MARY GILLILAND

CODHILL
PRESS

FURTHER PRAISE FOR *THE DEVIL'S FOOLS*

From the opening line, "We have plenty of stories," to the finale, Mary Gilliland's *The Devil's Fools* proves a wide-ranging narrative which incorporates tales from classical myth, the Bible, the speaker's daily life, set in a world eroticized yet also spiritual. Through her stories, Gilliland examines the tensions of heterosexual relationships, a search for the divine in contemporary life, mystery in the daily. This book is both journey and celebration, glowing and tender. In a poetry full of images from the physical world, nature around us and the body's earthliness, Gilliland gives us her "dirty yes to life."

> **Mary Crow,** Poet Laureate of Colorado,
> author of *I Have Tasted the Apple*

To see through Mary Gilliland's eyes is to experience afresh and anew the wonders of encounter with the liminal, the mysterious, and the all too ubiquitous but largely unseen. Enjoy the ride! As Gilliland calls us in Dionysus's voice, "Greet me by Apollo's marble door, Meet me where Artemis drops spoor, Find me in the shadows of reliefs." Indeed I will—and what a joy and journey awaits!

> **Heidi M. Ravven,** author of *The Self Beyond Itself:*
> *An Alternative History of Ethics, the New Brain*
> *Sciences, and the Myth of Free Will*

The
DEVIL'S
FOOLS

poetry by

MARY GILLILAND

c

CODHILL PRESS
NEW YORK • NEW PALTZ

CODHILL
PRESS

Codhill books are published by
David Appelbaum for Codhill Press

codhill.com

THE DEVIL'S FOOLS

Published in the United States of America

ISBN 978-1-949933-16-1
Library of Congress Control Number: 2022939012

Cover and Book Design by Jana Potashnik
BAIRDesign, Inc. • bairdesign.com

A. M. D. G.

CONTENTS

THE DEVIL'S FOOLS

For in my nature I quested for beauty but God, God has sent me to sea for pearls.

—Christopher Smart

THE WOMAN IN THE HAT PAUSED, MOLE-EYED

We have plenty of stories
The left side of the neck, the bottom of the big toe
A shadow in the garden, a prejudice against the wolf
Forward without hesitating, not knowing whither
Not there? Any more than here?
Then where is God?

We might be sick, blood loose in our entrails
The hard tread of conversation, for example
Within ourselves?
Nowhere?
Hastening upstairs, staring across at the window
Remembrance torn in the sea wind swiftly, blindly

LYRE

Life had, the astrologer said,
  but one curse: I could not
    go mad.

When I heard the music
  I cannot repeat
    I was halfway home
      five years into the voyage.

Their voices were honey
  measure by measure
    dropped on the small of my back.

I married the ropes
  as well as the mast
    my writhing as ranting
      a plea as my shouts.

      Today I recall not one word.

When I beached I made thanks.
  I walked home to the face
    without an adventure
      to which I was wedded.

GOD OF THE VINE

My followers seemed to be in motion,
their *mise en place*, revels: dance, torn throat.
My foot stretched with age. But I was stuck.

I am no cartoon, emerging
unscarred from the twirling, crafty endurance
of a character larger than life

and the devilish climates—blast, swelter,
damp, drought, frost—can be stoppers
of fracas, of chill generated from within.

My mother, a goner. Born in that clap
of illumination, I must tell you
my heart's true love was the quiet life.

I fainted on the donkey's back,
dreamed I was nursed in peace
as we crossed the river to Dodona

where the oracle crawls the plain
shock of oak leaves in autumn,
rattling tedium's brown racket.

PROSERPINE

I fell in with a man from a small country.
He stopped on a rainy lane and asked did I want a ride.
My mother'd told me always to follow my feet

but the fumes that day overpowered my nose.
He bit me hard then nubbed at my love pearl.
Red seeds fell from the wound. He says I ate them.

He offered me board if I paid for room
among bloodless artistes and ivory heroes
by charging his battery—one or two shocks.

Time passed and faded. There's a beauty in that.
He took up his helmet. I saw he was sightless.
I said let's let it rip. Soot fell about us.

Once I'd signed his note that hell could not be
improved on, he set me loose for the summer.
He'd have slipped me into his wallet if I'd fit.

THE FERTILE LAND

He doesn't say, but my growing thistle
does not capture the castle. One each year
to thrive where its seed set. This one

still branching and still growing in the shade
is higher than my husband's head. I promise
not to let it go to seed when he flies to

a place far far away. Then I wait.
Lying quiet, head bent, the pair of hills
rising from flat white expanse. Stroking them

myself. Thistle's down is silkier and stickier
than any other, striking on the stalk, hard
to see when fallen. Like the water bug in

the cleavers ointment, the web at dusk
across the threshold, the snake that speaks,
the water of life. Like Susanna Clarke's

Man with the Thistle-down Hair, who bewitches
English ladies in the wake of the Napoleonic wars
with a severed little finger or a log of

moss oak in a casket. Can Jonathan Strange
magically retrieve them for his wife and her
best friend and place them where they properly

belong? His way is eerie as the drift
of one strand floating from the mound,
his task to pluck before the down is down.

SLIP

The maker of my asymmetric kitchen bowls
regards them seconds. The lip of one
curves out, another up. Yet they nest,
a set for soup, for stir-fry hot with ginger
on half-lit days when rain astigmatizes

sight. Keats fears the clay of self-undoing
collapsed upon ambition's wheel
more than a name vanished, ink on water.
He knows abandon a more vibrant thing
than mere perfection, more

nourishing. Bowls rimmed with
vines distinctly green from which droop
purple-blue—wisteria bud? or grape?
This could be flower, could be fruit
blurs as though through watered glass.

DRENCHED

I drank to knock out the ego. I drank before
The breakers are strong today, the only option is to dive right into

I had to travel. I drank knowing I'd feel
their crests. There are just a few magenta jellyfish; the hordes that

seasick the next day. I drank when I felt
filled the sea last week have disappeared. I wish I could see

edgy around people. I drank to toast the
twenty-twenty for occasions like this. After swimming, I couldn't

first warm day of spring. I drank because my
even read lying under the beach umbrella; I could only watch and

first love blew me off. I drank because I was
listen to the surf. Twenty years since I've been in this ocean—how

angry. I drank because I was sexy and
healing it is. Maybe next summer I'll rent a house here. I hear

wanted to feel sexier. I drank in order to feel
gulls, geese, and for some reason a mourning dove. Aunt Lil said

any -er. I drank in order to stop feeling. I
"This is what they call a large day." Michael gave me a wet open

drank because I hated my father. I drank
baby kiss, the kiss of someone who hasn't got the pucker yet. Hot

because my father did. I drank because I had
drive to get here, discovering Route 10 isn't country anymore.

work to do. I drank because the work was
It's mallville, overcome with shoppers, the bulldozers still

done. I drank to be a poet. I drank because
humming. Parkway traffic backed up a mile each time we neared

>

I couldn't think of anything to write. I drank

one of the shore exits. Here. I'm here. You don't have to stand up

because I was in company. I drank because

to the ocean, you can let it carry you. A woman with a sunburned

I felt lonely. I drank because life was sad.

belly is being mothered by the sea; she rolls in the low surf as the

Life was happy. I drank to get drunk.

incoming tide enfolds her.

LIT WITH RADIANCE

Joy oscillates to sorrow as a dolphin
breathes one element to move in another,

as a butterfly eats the plant's green solids
when it crawls, the nectar when it's winged.

Sorrow fathoms glory as a tree's roots
curl irregular in shape and thickness,

unsteadying the outline of its trunk.
Glory rouses joy the way a mystery

comes close to shadow, or a shoulder
leads the knee from ground to space

where curvature saddles the known universe.
Joy announces sorrow in the wish to live

in many countries, turn all corners,
marvel at the streets, and wash them.

Sorrow ambers glory inside shabby rental houses,
motes of sunlight, pollen, shoes well broken in.

HOLY ISLAND

Am I hearing the split lauds of pilgrims
bent from hours on the motorway
fingering their maps? the causeway awash?

Do these hands nestle in pleasure
as twigs stirred by a breeze find the calm
of gravity? Arc lines in my palms
the branches of what I have sacrificed?

Twice daily the tide, hilling toward dune grass
covers the road to the mainland.
Grass—clear page on a still day,
a scribble when the gale blows off the sea.

The Lindisfarne monks stirred pigments they ground
from earth's plants and metals
through the manuscript tracing Jerusalem's news,
the tree, the lamb, the vine.

Hands cupped on thighs in a sanctuary
unroofed long ago, I stand beneath
a thin red arch of sandstone thumbed by wind.

Miniature daisies scatter a white toehold.
Sound thrums through space to this green place,
this clapper in the bell wanting heaven.

ROSSLYN CHAPEL'S ARTISANS

1. The Master

Let there be an upright. Let corbels keep
the upright wedged, stone perpendiculars
against its stone, pure shaft and bar, that and
this: a man is angled, faced; his soul
form without error. To found a town he plants a cross
over a mouthless spring, then has a girl
entice a dragon there: wrathful fire tamed
heralds agriculture—charms the plants to stay.

Across our landscape appear faces: gods
that Nature keeps unseen. Just so, the work
of masons is the absence of our shape.
One reaches only once;
see that you reach far. Pin the dragon
on the path. Carve a roof—a vaulted
groin, with roses, leaves and stars.

For the greater glory of our God, let
your pillar uptake dragons and spew vines.
Inset between squared corners, from capital
to base as though a cloth had unrolled of
itself, a diptych of this pattern:
Meld cockleshell with fleur-de-lis, and crush.
Knot round and round a space where they are not.

Let the pillar support child and lovers,
marksman, builder, planter, pruner. Carve next
to each the fleshless bones. Top the whole with an angel
holding spread book, empty page. Your work scribes
within the stone what appears not there—names
that keep men going and bring them back.
Resist the blasted barren mind's soliloquy:
No one can be saved. No one can be kept.

2. The Mother

Stop rattling my door. I've worked my dusty
shift within the shop of the divine,
trued the wheel and dressed the block until it
worked me doubletime. I haven't energy
to carve a roast. The kettle's on, fire
banked, my hammer's misplaced, apron gone.
Your brisk fist pounds the casing, then thumbs
worry the lock: my fingers agitate
with the wounds that tools heft from an untouched
surface. Upon the pillar's opaque
capital, you'll want hewn and bound a ram
and sacrificial boy, bearded father
with a knife. You'll want a Green Man close by,
his tongue a vine scrolling the chapel wall,
lithe serpents twined about the column's base,
ropes of foliage wound up the shaft.
Last time I fell in love it tore me so
I kept it to myself. Reach? Draft someone
else. I live with a silent chisel, rasp
and file laid side by side. Tether not this
dragon, unremarked, unseen——

——As I reach
the sided stone rounds, topped with openwork.

3. The Apprentice

No template carved this capital: angelic
implements unfix—scroll there, here bell
or shield. Or it withstands the angels:

ram, fruit, roses are its crown; the cockle
shell, the flux of stars patter in rounded rows,
pattern unset, the emblems variant.

One long neck with wings, eight dragons
set their tail in mouth, a base that firms
the pillar, a cross-stitch for a column

ribbed like a fall of frozen water,
an artery of ironed hair. But see
the four strands in relief that writhe it:

stranded curves of fruitless foliage,
double spirals, differing like the mismatch
in the germ on which matching depends.

On which the universe depends, the dance
that splices dancers. Why does one helix
fold another in its spin? Plasm, eyeless

gropes toward its new fate. The way a trampled
dragon might meet a wounded saint.

CONVERSE

Scout of the movement of sky, our man works the field.
He bends to examine the row, clumped with dung from the bull,
hand in the grainsack that falls with his shoulder.

Parsifal ambles toward the horizon. White breakers kneel
on the blue of the sea. His sack is a fool's toggle slung round
his neck, his fate a hag on a horse instead of an income.

Would that grail had the substance of grain! he cries to the farmer.
The muffled return: *Spur your own flanks, not the horse's.*

Each clutches whinstone, earth's molten core
fissured through limestone, pooled, cooled and chipped:
a piece of a wall or philosopher's stone or dear
animosity. Would that shadow could predicate mirror.

NO OUTLET

Bend down to see it:

The skeleton wades from the west
through stubble picked clean
by a farmwife contending with fieldwise geese.

The boy faces east, away from the reaper
toward the learning of learning
at ease in his mother's lap.

Her finger outlines the letter,
his lips make the o, the vellum
he sees hammered with flowers.

The mid-figure balances
one foot on empty circle,
one on filled globe

as though hoop and ball
would not roll, roll
nor mother's name liven stone.

Ascend—by Rosslyn's pilgrim-worn stairs
from the fourteenth century workshop—
to the infinite wrinkle of chiseled stone:

Verticals, vaulted ceiling, nearly every pillar
carved with figure or design, two stories above
earls in the crypt interred naked in their armor—

and the last mason's mallet buried in the chapel wall.

CAIN

Angst has never been other than sweet
atop tumuli worn with eons of rains'
gravity bundling the hours.

How birds homed in that first time
from every direction. An unhurried mist
cracked the tumult of branch.

The taste has not changed. I leave him
unburied wherever he lists. Lance this
stripling wind. Unsheathe the blast.

MIDLOTHIAN

Clocks addled, wandering in long daylight to land's end
where the Esk bends, we skip rocks, pile a cairn

of granite, sandstone, bits of glass, pocky curves, striped shards —
a river's take from igneous hills where hide, flesh, bones are stilled.

On Whitsunday along the prime meridian, churchwalls muffle
prayer for farmer suicides, for split hemispheres of shepherd

sheep. Diggers trench field-long graves. Air transports a relentless slurry.
Thistled clearances hold burning flocks. *Led by an invisible hand* firm as

stones that incomers might pitch or cradle in, townsfolk
and villagers roll towels, stuff thresholds, lintels, jambs.

QUARANTINE IN THE BORDERS

there is a tendency　　Of each physiological variable
Research funding to continue　　*a flippancy generated*
what is the second sin　　Rapid eye movement (REM) sleep
And infrared lights　　*I struggle so much*
handle all ten commandments　　Over a 24h period
The simultaneous electromyogram　　*with this curious property*
Of the technique　　Of sleep in sheep

competition among tour groups　　The first stage
Information is collected　　*bigger faster engines*
higher speeds increasing traffic　　Surface skin electrodes
EEG, EOG, EMG and video　　*struck and killed*
watched in horror　　Sleep analysis software
Results from this work　　*going to see more of?*
(Frequency and amplitude)　　Wind wind Swept swept Farm

Stay away from sheep　　*shot forth on my back*
through the air　　Please help to contain
The current outbreak　　*awarded honorary degrees*
where does this go?　　Do not leave any litter
Keep dogs on lead　　*my own brand of laziness*
a perfectly useless bit　　That part of the earth

'TO ASHES . . . TO DUST'/
THE CATTLE OF THE SUN

Say we were redeemed from myth,
mouthing vernacular:
Lamb of God, grant us peace.

Now conflate fact and figure:
ecumenical animal sacrifice
in the fields of France, across Britain.

The hymnal held the translation
while a priest thumb pressed our foreheads.
His Latin flavored the phrase,
kept what it meant an eon away.

One Wednesday a year we looked smudged,
perhaps smug, jumping rope after Mass,
taking a turn at the red wooden handle
contesting devoutness amid counting rhymes: who could

keep her medallion of ash through the classroom,
the bedsheets, the breakfast next morning?
who could remember to not wash her face?

Let's say the herd is held in common,
that no one pilfered the field
of golden-tongued uncle Apollo.
Commerce has no god uncle,
strums no tortoiseshell lyre.

Hermes flies swift as thought
foot in mouth, disinfected.
Let's say slaughter.
       Slaughter
Slavery.
       Slay
forty thousand per diagnosed case.
Let's give up meat for Lent.

Trade.
        Trade
let us say, let us pray.
Steep
        and Sterile
the ashes fall down.

Pyres burn for the trickster,
the god with winged sandals.

        Multiply them
by ten.
        Again
                says the toddler
        who stole
the cattle of the sun.

WAKE ME

In the treeless light of Delos
mullein flowers burn round
and the stone lions
have waited so long
some have lost their smiles,
others their heads.

In Eleusinian bus exhaust
rain beads like wax
drops along a candle
toward the smashed ruins.

In Samaria the temples
are not slabs of stone.
Water cold as fire
channels the gorge.

In the neglect at Dodona
Persephone has burned
to a shade thinner than sorrow
and fled to the caverns
leaving a painted turtle
to stare down the lizards.

DIONYSUS

Greet me
  by Apollo's
      marble door
Meet me
    where Artemis
        drops spoor

Find me in the shadows of reliefs

Bind me
in the narrows
wide with grief

Trust me when you've outlived hell
          and boneset flowers black

A steady fall:
        your snowflake cell
            my Himalayan back

THE WILD CELERY

Now you fear joy—as though a flattened hybrid
could sate appetite, green that was its origin
bleached nearly white.

Hot-housed, plastic-bagged—will that be
the meal? or what grows in the marsh,
its mud-flanged heart.

Eat your peck of dirt your mother heard
her mother say, the soup free of purity's
temporary money.

You've trimmed house, pruned career, composted
old griefs. The first seasoning recorded
was celery's bitter leaf.

Your hands will lever from a final bed, elbows angle
like a flail. Where tight ribs meet on a tough stalk
your finger traces insect trails to the crease.

INTERMITTENT PIPE

Cutworm, aphid, weevil, earwig
Let go your fruits, your fondnesses, your friends
Dial tone, click, unexpected knock, voice override
Let go your agenda, your hoarse throat, your interruption
Sun, clear air, warm earth
Let go your habitation, your namesakes, your flag
Button, tatting, pocket, dart, pleat
Let go your edger, your embroidery
Wisdom, order, peace, heart
Let go your hampers
Clarity, thoroughness, good will
Let go your holding back
Fanbelt, cylinder, regulator, winch
Let go your alternator
Katydid, mantis, soldier bug, lady beetle
Let go your sawfly, your leafroller, melon worm
Measles, ague, plague, melanoma
Let go your bathroom, grocery, your druggist
White clover, hairy vetch, buckwheat, spring oats
Let go your summer cover
Give up your hair, your nail nipple elbow
Key, awl, Allen wrench, icepick, hanger
Give up your worship, your worry, workload, world
Cloverleaf, rotary, roundabout
Let go your going
Heatwave, snowsquall, typhoon, sirocco
Dry your hair
Sten gun, repeater, tank, stripes, grenade
Sing your ballad, your sources, your harmonics
Fly on (your) lacewing, curl in (your) welkin
Bridge, dike, aqueduct, rampart
Let go your reign, your levy, patrol

HEAT WAVE

Pools of rubber bands, staples, tape—tools
that anchor small pieces of circumstance—
still the left drawer. The right swells with
burnt memos clipped, blank index cards.

A mosquito netter flutters the corner
bewildered in its search for food.
Shelves hold hollyhock buds from Delphi,
serpentine from California, a double sailor's knot.

There's much to do and no call to do it,
nothing to breathe or suck, no blade to
shave this callus, nothing to despair of.
Devil on left shoulder breaks a pencil.

Idleness works up defiance, entices
God to sweat—the devil's fool.
Moist forearms peel the map of the oak desk.
Astrolabe and compass slip their anchors.

AMONG THE TREES

— Genesis 3:8

When I ask *who are you?*
    the man calls noootelllinng
    as he leaps flights of stairs
        Lush greenery about a big house
        He is tugging so hard
    All I've managed to lock
    is the screen door
    with its old wooden slats
        There is nothing solid between us
    My foot braces the doorframe
    next to my hand on the latch
        He can see
        what he wants

The leaves smell of mustard and honey
as we snip spurred nasturtiums
fill a basket with trophies
        tangerine, scarlet, salmon, gold flowers
        and cascading green shields
to thicken the soup

                Wind tears the flume of burning oil
                to a flock
            tomorrow's black rain on the desert
        Trained on speed and porn
          they zip their jackets in the dawn
      The pilots wedge a swift passage
      of markings on the sky
    an alphabet

We come home from a Sunday swim
    in the sticky heat
      when everyone's away

and we? we screw twice before discovering
an old-fashioned rubber window stop
beneath the reading chair
  The lock
   between top and bottom sash
   sheared
the storm window snug on the houseface
refitted
its eyes hooked to exterior trim
   Nothing stolen
But you set ten-penny nails in the casing
three inches above the bottom pane
   so we can ventilate
   and still protect ourselves

      There will be no more lies declares Boris
     The iron curtain is torn
      And Natasha?
    Oil and wood
     scarce as winter leaves
     change hands
   Grandmothers sift
    through the rubbish bins
Thugs price the bread

When the air is still
and fledgling robins
anchor fat bellies to warm grass
   lay their beaks on the earth
   arc their feathers like a blessing
we pause in our weeding near the tree
whose roots kill the trees around it

      I garden in the shade on rock
     transplant mullein, trellis pokeweed
   The bulbs for this place
are a tall order

                 >

The woman is a fascinating talker
Her words feel like someone
washing my hair
I will never make
my dinner date on Skull Street
with the pale young man
who has a crush on me
I am spellbound
by the many rooms in her mansion
rooms to let
and their sliding dream doors
reminiscent of the entrance
to the Steel Pier arcade:
the clown's mouth

Exposed in your element
tellurian
you're so free as you sleep

At the summer lath house
in the Sierra foothills
the cat's feet
thump the boards of the deck
while my shirt passes over my head
The shorts leave my fingers
just before I glimpse
the tiny goldfinch
fly from her mouth
when fabric hits fur

Animal in a borrowed bed
I wake to arms I cannot see
a torso not a memory
nor your imprint
but harbor I've not felt
since reaching the age of reason
A guardian, those wings

Stormwind bends the branches like magma
        like meteors
        a carpet of diamond
        a mare's tail

Layer, flesh

Love is faulty
Love is blind . . .

One day
we have guests at the houseboat
A dear old friend
and the woman he wants
to be   the
                woman
                in a long series of these
                        This
                        woman
                takes us
                to an estate planted with camellias
                        hilly acres
                        silky color
and she has snakey hair
He
is an amateur photographer
with a pro's ability
to catch the light
When the camera catches me
in the galley at the foldup table
back at the boat
                after we light the kerosene lamps
                        I flicke

Your cock is like wallpaper
part of everyday around the household

To see New York!
Or Rome

>

                              Our guide to Corinth
                         a schoolteacher who managed
                    to send her son to college
                         in America
                    tells us the site's entire history
                         mythic and recorded
                              from the Stone Age to Byzantium
                              in under 30 minutes
                                        loves best with her wise voice
                              the missionary Paul
                         who preached on the spot
                    where our feet stand
                    and was not heeded

Most of her few listeners   Across the Peloponnese
from that country   above Hera's colossal head
that her son embraces   and her sole standing column
make loud jokes   the first Olympic runners
about the Roman potties   run

Startled in the garden
a furry poacher
slinks furtively, greedily
through flowers and beans
          creeps through the Havahart
          swipes the lettuce
                    Her siblings clap their backs
                    on the sides of the openwork steel cage
                    in their transport to a country field

          Under sweeping sun
          in a posted world
          she rises on hind legs
          sniffs a thin silence
                    No, we are wrong clots my throat
                    with the .22's report

Between the dream of the man
and the dream of the woman
meteors showered
We stood with hands on hips
each other's hips
the stars soft and bright
with dust

As my shape changed
as I grew out
I stood before a full-length mirror
and pulled my thin nightgown
around my waist
and revealed, revealed
In childhood
I balanced
on the maple bedpost
on my *umbilicus*

face down, the palms of my feet
on a low bureau

I liked the hurt
I called it
Captain Hook

Scarlet
strapless

tossed underwear

Marriage starts
with a veil

Hi honey
with a hammer and a credit card

Sometimes
us male nudes
just take what we want   >

Vacuuming the rubble
between men and women
forces the dust up
  We sack housecleaning
  chop vegetables for soup

    Bomb after bomb
   protects the American right
  to drive the Caprice Classic
Our neighbor washes his car
with Sunday love

Thinking there's knowing
in a *spinus erectus*
people stand
for a lot of things

Trying to love you better—

  Carnival glow
  lights workworn faces
  brings crowds to the floodlights
  strung before the old church
  Marimbas crescendo
  then silence
  steady as grazing cattle
  holds the dancers
  in their yellow blouses
  The flutist bows
  to those eating shrimp
  by the bandstand
  On the margin of the square
  green eyeshadow
  smeared on her cheek
  a solitary dancer
  steps
  in the irremediable wind
  of drunkenness
    You touch my hand
     in the dark of the theatre
    You open
     a door in my chest

Love's a maker
Love's a kind
of thunder approaching
in the cool of the evening
bidding, forbidding
to ignite
among the trees of the garden
(I've filled my hand)
upright sleek miracles

SABBATH

If I pause about my business
you ride me. How could a soul
be bold enough to forego such
sex on short notice? They would
have to wash dishes, face mortality
and testimonials at the door.
Meanwhile we grow not old & frail
but old and sore. Here we go
again putting on our clothes today.

As I watch disappear
there where you smell like bread rising
—and here where it starts to get
interesting, I'm afraid you will say
the wrong thing—which is anything
said—so before you consider what's next
my hands boom across the room
again, dear, a glorious 'gain.

SYNERGY

1

We'll marry, unfurl a continent
of longing, hum and storm
a canyon to the sea, lean
—blown pines—salted.

Dolphins ride the horses of the waves
before the diving pelicans or terns
or herring gulls can band about.

We watch them play
along the coast road to L.A.
in gray the sky makes
before it releases morning.

The dolphins stream like sand
through tides of light and hunger.

2

To be married is to edge pines brinked
tomorrow, is to bear the past, to live
—cracked glass—in the sharpest
meadow.

Mustangs jump the ocher-spotted crags.
Kites and kestrels, eagles
spread the air to join them.

We know their urge
to unleash time, space's verge
in sun's last red on curves
around the eyrie.

The horses lean like willows
in breeze of thirst and rustle.

>

3

To marry is to commit an act of
lunacy that nobody should wish on
you but always does, is to like angels
carve the firmament.

Thoughts evolve the irritants that fray
life's jacket and the threads that ravel death's
fine get-up, sanity's glad rags.

We feel their trace
upon the flesh of morning's race
through kisses, body fluids
and catastrophes of clothes.

Crooners of the spectrum and the storm
finance our drafts of love and going.

WE LIVE IN SYN CHRONICITY

There are treasure
hunts I make that
leave you scaven
ging for stimu
lation; your cap
acity to
be a captive
of the screen leaves
me unmoved. There
are days we have
no wishes for
each other, just
commands, forget
ting the unique
ness of our hist
ry. You crave a
ttention and mag
azine displays,
I approval
and tax rebates.

Will the gods in
side your flickring
box or mine be
hind the tree cut
us a little slack?
Fate's single-roofed
our duplex roosts
separate but e
qual. And yearning
for one body?
Our private ef
forts look like wil
full acts and spir
tual alibis.
Let's wage domes
tic profit, o
verlapped in time.
If you would clean
the ceilings I'
ll consider floors.

NO, BUT I GOT THE LAUNDRY DONE

Did you pick up your room?
Decide on vacation?
Did you finish the work
you brought home from work?

Remember to eat?
Feed mother her banana?
For a minute did you sail away
to just meditate?

Did you roll the conundrums
of life and of earth on your tongue?
Tip your hat? Buff your boots?
Sign a check that saves no one?

How does it start, the unreasoned conclusion?
... *In today's society, our frantic pace* ...
Were you asked in the hall, on the street
... *Can you stop a minute? Are you fair?*

And that real toad in your garden
—the hefty one who rose unblinking
on your new spring spade—
you did bow—*but to kiss it?*

WHY SHE CAN'T EAT THE LIGHT

1

Her first prisms are the cut-glass dangles
hooked by wire to a candleholder
on the highboy in their dark back room.

Sunlight would throw rainbows through the clear spears
if it had a moment here, if more than
an alley ran between the streets of rowhouse.

Her hand covers half a petal of one
flower on the rug. Moving Not the icy prisms
Not my daughter But Mommy surely is.

The clank of knives on plates of Sunday lamb
interrupts the conflict hung with silence.
Green mint jelly is spooned into her mouth.

2

When the candlesticks join Hummels and milk glass
in her mother's bright suburbia
she pokes and watches patterns arc like swings.

Her father's beryl eyes furrow a field
without a playground, entrained at eight then
back at six, hours without apprehension.

The absence of a wavelength shows as color.
Mother has transparent faith but red words
shell his tidy drying of the dishes.

The old people are dead, the rowhouse sold.
Why she can't eat the light could puzzle her.
The prisms burn in a room called dining.

>

3

If she had a daughter, what would name her?
The crystals knock in heat from a wood fire,
heave their cup of light to multicolored shards.

Hushed thuds—the cat darts paws as if to snare
a bird. Like the wall behind the pattern
she has absorbed all colors but her own.

She has moved her mother's move from family
further than her grandmother would want to know
—or her father fathom—to upstate hills.

At least the man that she can blame in love
or work talks louder. It's pity or
self-pity, no one delicate along.

SHE WANTED MY HEARTS
THE SAME WAY

She once said of the boys *their equipment is exposed,*
such a vulnerable way to go through life.

She tumbled me the way the waves do seastones.
Me then nine others, eight of us full term.

Brim of her womb I sit wearing her ULTIMATE HAT™.
Rainable, sunable, crushable, still like new.

The table silvered wood, bench damp.
The line for fried sweet dough not getting any shorter.

A child paws rhinestone at the tideline.
Three in diapers and me tall enough to help.

The rhythm of that house was frantic—
tripping on, pulling, red wagons, plastic cups.

Her emeried nails—*they were mother's! I can't*
help it—lined up my earlobe's notched opal studs.

With a stroller at a crosswalk, there was my pebble
of a voice—Wait little ones—until the light changes—

GOING PLACES

And if I had chosen my locale
by answering the nation's classifieds
as though the soul, my only daughter,
could be left behind, its yearning
a music that fate disallowed?

Spring song nips from a high snag,
the ending notes soft red arrows
pricking the roots' dusk.
The Devil stops with his bag of gold,
wants only one thing in return.

Hands in pockets, I would likely
learn to thrive where circumstance set me,
sea wind woven in my cloth, or desert sun.
But I've raindrop on rock thirty years,
the wormy old apple dropping its fruit.

THE ADVERSARY

It's Satan writes the lines for Faust
whose mentor in crime
invented crime, whose *I will not
serve* under the alias Lucifer
bore him into a role eternal—
all the world the Devil's platform.

We give him no billing
on the marquee, no neon
bulbs spell out his name. But
he's everywhere—underground
as though injected into basalt
to mineralize, about to sprout
the tastebuds of his ready tongue—
if we slip off our earbuds
—perhaps if we slip them on!—

Faust might get the billing
but a hapless man's movements hardly matter.
He'll go out the way he came in.
Remember Frankenstein the scientist?
Frankenstein registers
in our roster
the monster.

THE WAY I TALK

Anyone who overheard would wink you up a tree
or think our loving could be spared
my going at you on a bare trail in the wood.

You did not woo this banshee.

You cameo'd a smiling girl to spend steady days with,
got tangled with my scrimshaw toes
looping the strand of upstate winters.

That night of frozen broccoli and cod, port,
Forbidden Planet, my apartment-mate off
on a fly-golf week, I called work—
that I was snowed in.

Impulsive, you thought my routine. I spent years
scraping through snow no one else manufactured.
You gave up telling me to stop.

Worse was the early sobriety, years of it
drunk on the gravelly voices of obvious men.

Now that's done, you have my Irish tongue—
rage at all that's gone over the sea, under the hill
centuries of word sharp as briar in mist.

GROWTH RINGS

What happens in the margins matters
Each of us nurses ragged edges

Greening's undergone during months without
the we that breakless days would spoil

Last night I foresaw the fester, being left
I lay awake to listen to your breath

Shall I bandage today's flight, swab tomorrow?
Or is what's needed fire starter?

I dreamt I split the kindling in the walls
The wood with stares and pats undid the split

Finger on a bare tree's sap's not languor
Nor is crushing dry leaves sorrow

WINTER IN THE GARDEN

When I squat to the spade base, the handle does the lifting
so I see the yellowed body in cascades of loosened earth.

With the blind human movement toward the future
my pointer finger tucks the damp sack of her belly.

A webbed foot rests on clods of grubs
and buried eggs whose hatch will wake her.

With the half-mew of a cat moved from an easy chair
the toad rebukes me in her dreaming.

BLACKBILLED CUCKOO

Freedom wags. The everyday
turns up a shimmering trail,
brushes a rain net on your coat.
The woods are wet, will grow.
Call gorge meltwater: overflow.
Call buds from the branch's
patient winter stand: sap inkles green.

Color of hope, its becoming
lights on your head.
You speak in tongues
and amaze those who missed
your red eye, who thought your dun back
a bough crystalled in ice
too taut with beauty to change.
Caterpillars break out.
You rave.

DOG DAY HARVESTFLY

Clamped upon ribbed ridges
where shell cracked a central seam
the full-grown harvestfly emerges aqua
lighter blue than anywhere in nature,
two three-inch wings
spread not yet for flying
drying.

To the brown shell of a nymph
that grubbed on root juices three years
—whose empty feet
will grip the cohosh leaf
until the next great wind—
clings the origin of faerie.
To a dull mound with emptied legs.

When peach juices and blackberry
run down the chin and a dozen
ears of corn tassel market sacks
we see them parked on flagstones
or outgreening the grass,
black back and eyes, clear wings
with emerald hems, and the red shoes

of creatures who have longed
to dance, whose feet will never cross
church threshold, whose bread of life
is air. In an hour the spread wings
will shutter the great body,
vibrant vulnerable blue
hardening before the rain.

LARGER THAN LIFE

. . . get you, my pretty! . . . have what she's having . . .
. . . red pill or blue pill . . . together and blow . . .
The greatest actors have no ideas of their own.

They're like the caps we love sliced raw with spinach
or fried in butter, slight pressure from the teeth on the omelette's

fungal fruit as we bite without much or any thought
to the mycelium net beneath the ground, its tremendous job
of organizing life on this planet.

Frankly, my dear . . . nobody's perfect . . . round up the usual suspects.
Mushrooms concentrate nutrition. Mushrooms consume substances
toxic to other life. They *come up and see us sometime.*

BECAUSE IN THE LEAFPILE
I PITCHFORKED
A YELLOWJACKET NEST

Bites on my body I can stand, but not on yours.
Like anyone I think I'm built to last.
But I can't articulate your false step
nor right the ladder, level the tipped motorbike.

A few welts on you scar me with gravity:
agonizing seizures from a mistaken backyard herb,
lightning-detonated newly-painted house
the evening I stay late at the office.

Thumbs of fire massage my back
as I run across the lawn, stripping the shirt
that presses like a sheet against me.
You ice the wounds. They do not swell.

I propose to feed my back to angry bees
then to their grandsons, their great-grandsons:
take this red flesh instead of my love's body.
Prickled and confused, I straighten up.

There was that winter Saturday, that
dusk the afterimage of a Frankenstein matinee
when the top row in the cemetery wall stretched
stone points level with my cat-eyes.

I'd walk back and forth, back and forth.
The hand sliding over the jagged spikes paused
a fingerprint from the skin of my neck
knuckling limbo, neither movement nor dirt.

NEMESIS

The burdock no one dug for spring tempura
or a boast of victory over taproot
leafs out vast and ribbed. Its stalk
crests the human head, blossoming magenta.

During August the young burr scratches
shoulders, teases clothes. Mercy will vanish
as it dries and the winds whisper
a pox on the horse's tail, the neat edge of a lawn.

Persistent as shark or cockroach
burdock remembers ferns high as trees,
brontosaurus necks lengthening until their pea-heads
could chew enormous fiddleheads, sharp cold

or claws sudden in the belly bringing them to earth.
In daylight and darkness throughout nature's
mammal dreams, burdock heard first the apes
who walked, sure they would wear the crown.

ABOUT TO BURN HER DRESS

Where has she been this sweltering day
since she paused beside the horsehair armrest
and interrupted Mr. Borden's nap

then glided by the kitchen where the maid
was plunged into a sticky business—canning—
and picked her way out to the shed?

The nimbus clouds cut open.
The sluice dulls her scarlet apron.
Crystals pitter patter on her nose.

Or is the cloudburst something that
like so much else only her farfetching
imagination sees? Fall River slips away

—the shed's wood floor, the ax, the open door.
Lizzie's willowy, an orphaned flower in the yard
and done with papa's snores from the settee.

Empty eyes raised to cold heaven, she stalks
the plank that keeps her long skirt from
fresh puddles on her way back to the house.

STIRRINGS

Mother spends nights on her feet
tipping pills into throats of the aged,
swabbing their bedsores, chucking wet linen,
the rotator cuff hurling pain's metal
the length of her arm.
At mid-shift, at three, at the gooseneck lamp
lighting her station, she writes up the charts.

In the mornings, sleepheavy,
she wheedles her daughter's pressed thumbs
from the abdomen under the nightie,
guides them to the pitcher's handle,
slides the cereal under the milk
and with luck holds her tongue at bodily
nonsense, the girl nine years old.

She takes off her nurse's uniform
and slides into bed, the man turning his back,
hands balled in the clamp of his knees.

CRITICAL MASS — DISPOSED OF

For years I heard confusion clap its bell:
audience waiting on my words, choice

speech trapped in a splay throat. You
weren't quite balanced when you fashioned

punishment: a ragged two-by-four across
my cotton underpants. I had warned my friend

—Presbyterian—she was on her way to hell.
Corrected! my first chance to pipe our

church's spell. Old man, today I cradled pulsars
—compassion turned toward me—and talked

memory drift aloud. The steady on-off
beating through my fingers cleared it—out.

THE BARGAIN

I forgive the young doe for eating the blackeyed susans,
for hosta tops bitten just as the flowerheads formed.
So intelligent—she waited for the sweetest mouthfuls.

She's the first deer to stand, to let me sing to her.
A few brief chews, then she lifts her head like a bird,
walks off calmly into the woods after swallowing fallen pears.

This is a good house. We let out a milksnake curled in the basement
and moved in. Five years ago a stag browsed six-foot burdock.
Above their spikes antlers rose before he bolted.

The animals go before us, prints marking woods edge and trail
and the fair trade of the forest: lettuce and green beans.
Fence wire bends where cleft hooves sank, darkening moist loam.

SCOTTISH ROOTS

I had wondered
      why on earth
the British count it
      among the trees.
Now, as it helps me
      climb rockface
to the left
      and keeps me from
nettle on the right,
      I know.

I know, too, its growth
      of six years
keeps concealed, keeps
      me from finding
the cave—really
      more a broad
opening—we reached,
      feet upon another's
shoulders, heads slid in
      to look up.

Legs dangling
      out of sandstone,
noses stuffy with
      dust, we could see
the S spiral, the circle
      within circles,
the series of triangles
      and figures that
might or might not
      stand for humans.

The Pictish carvings I'm
      looking for—signs
of my ancestors'
      ancestors—hidden now

—have found their way
          to another place.
Rooks nest overhead.
          The river below
lofts over the rocks
          and under.

Perhaps my descendants
          are hexing my eyes,
haunting the ravine
          already, small
in the cranesbill popping
          through forget-me-not
while my vigorous feet
          hide in ropes
hands cliff climb,
          leaves of vine.

MOTHERWORT

As forest green leaves reverse in wind
dusty silver undersides' veins bulge.

Embryonic rings of spurred seeds
halt hand's slide at intervals
along the tall four-sided stalk.

Leonurus cardiaca has a robin
sherwood shine, a slightly darker slightly
danker nature than its fellow weeds.

Minute orchids top the taloned
seedcrowns—frillpink visors.

Whence the fomentative power
—plucked, bruised, steeped—
to break fever, lift childbirth cramp.

MY DIRTY YES TO LIFE

At what point now does saying No
redeem a girl? The long consequence
of Catholic education is not fear of hell

or waking late but that spent agility.
When I eat no meat on Friday no soul
exits Purgatory. No necking and no petting

nor just how far to go was ever fun
among the paralyzing imprint of purloined
Hebrew metaphor—lost sheep, prodigal sons.

I failed to arrive where manna showered
nor did I strike water from a rock
nor Goliath with one. My faith in miracles

runs to the chance panting extreme unction
where, absolved, I'll nod off without sin
alongside the flaw that makes loss worth singing.

A Philistine inclines over girlhood's shards,
hosts of torn love letters dusting the way down.

YOUR MOUTH ON ME

Six clean-stitched blue-molded inches cover
pelvic bone to crotch. You drop by, see
me dress, in shorts nearly fabricless—
no cuffs or back pockets. Gypsy slips
into the summer. In a handspan's
denim, I walk along beside you
down the trail to frame a neighbor's window.

We'll elude at parties the stunned mates that
we arrive with, ditch bonfire for woods . . .
Vapor rises from my sturdy forearms to
the mountain air; aureoles meander from
soaked hair as I step from an outdoor sauna.
If it were fired up there would be others
there, communal Sundays. I am
alone, sponge-rinsed and nearly dry
when you come looking for an extra hand.

I am a woman who frames windows, hoists
a maul, whose waist stays small. Your lathe
smoothes the rings of crosscut antler
when I marry. As your eight-year-old sits
in the back, your palm slides from the stick shift
to me. He's not to know about the moment
you and I . . . the openwork of metal eyes
clasps the denim's nickel-sized front buttons.

If I leave the shorts draped on the sauna
rack, if I stay behind the door when
you call Anybody here? . . . I don't. I step and
stand there naked as a burnished violin.
I slip the short shorts up my thighs.
When the window's framed you slowly take apart
the halter top, a backless slip of red
that covers less of me than my long hair.

I pass along the shorts to my trim painter
a month after you die though as I stuff
them in her kit I do not know you have.
She inherits twenty-something years of
paint splats, wear marks, tears, hard gobs of roof
cement, top button etched with Wrangler.
She is rivetted, well toned, two months
from her due date. Then they'll fit.
When I give something away I see it.

FRESH COFFEE AFTER YOU ARE GONE

There's studied madness in opening bills after breakfast,
signing bank transfers. I clear my mind enough to know

a fallen stick of incense won't burn the house,
to figure out the cassette's lack of sound, the rasp

of its rotation, is my error not the answering machine's;
side A not B is the voice, still there, metallic

in the renovated room without its furniture:
I'll be he-e-re—the abecedarian of 4 AM—

*I know: Dinner time's the best time. Talk to
you later*—the manic laugh, disintegration after

successful surgery inside the frontal lobe.
Pick up. Pick it up! I am healed. Oligodendro-

glioma spreads its treeroots in the brain. If I
could have work to do, take aspirin and move on

instead of staring at the sad museum pieces
that pondering sculpts from love, as though understanding

were a place to live. If I could simply talk about
the damp closet upstairs, the milky trail of mildew

on black velvet, the yellowed dry cleaning tags.
Is the number on the scrap of paper 6 or 9?

As though knowing would be alchemy? Square one:
hot bitter brew, then the nothing that has to be done.

For an agitated hour I bundle one towel about
another in a ball, sort the light fabrics from dark.

AIR

A paper skim of ice on mud crunches underfoot;
watercress is thawing in the ditchside stream.
A cardinal has caught the sun. I have been ill, unthinking;
you have unhooked restraints with tenderness.

Parted and simple as the dark edge of wings
my hands sense an air hardly breeze, hardly wind,
that they sensed at Delphi after cold days of rain:

not the greenest god whose form is caught
in bronze in the museum, not the Castalian spring's
cold voice, not the scent of laurel burning in the tripod

but a pause between the charioteer's breaths,
a shudder as the harpstring comes to rest.

You walk me to the treasure, a sunlit drumlin
ridge called Dragon's Back, by the brushy path
below, lined with the spider's honied web.
I am mended with a newly ground desire:
able to receive. I lie down to be loved.

THE LANGUAGE OF BEES

On the rooftop garden
over the gallfly's home
the baldfaced hornet sips nectar.
The shag rug of florets covers her feet.

Mated already, surviving,
she'll overwinter in litter
then pulp wood in her mouth
for a pendant gray paper nest.
The larvae will close their own cells.

The year carries its freight,
its September. At the gambrel
of goldenrod plumes, she rocks
in the sun, pine fragrance stirring.
The slick yellow and black
stripes of her abdomen pulse,
bent to her mouth music.

MIGRATION

Geese knock dry cold in the stubble, clap upward.
Eve's foot pierces the edge of the garden.

Light is what she needs, not this
journey through temporal gloam
on a horse in the dark without reins.

                    That heady feeling:
Come along, come be born—

Someone's dreaming her now, a whir
like a buzz saw against time's grain.
The geese cry out, announce themselves

                    —cleave the Making.

NOTES

Lyre
Homer's 'wily Odysseus' spent 10 years wandering home to Ithaca from the Trojan War.

Proserpine
Although I prefer Greek names for mythic deities, the attitude of this poem's speaker begged for her Roman appellation.

The Fertile Land
Susanna Clarke's magical world of a novel is *Jonathan Strange & Mr Norrell*.

Rosslyn Chapel's Artisans
Faces of the apprentice, his mother, and his master are carved in the ceiling of Rosslyn Chapel, built in Midlothian, Scotland in the latter part of the 15th century. Three pillars toward the front of the chapel are known in esoteric masonry as Strength, Wisdom and Beauty. One is attributed to a master mason, another to his apprentice who (like Talos, the pupil of Daedalus whose work excelled his teacher's) was said to have been slain in a jealous rage. The middle pillar is unattributed, the only one of Rosslyn's 16 pillars not described in several centuries of detailed guidebooks.
This poem is for our mothers.

No Outlet
The 17th century carved ashlar is said to be known as 'King of Terrors.'

Midlothian
Written in memory of Britain's 2001 Foot-and-Mouth epidemic. Italicized words are from Adam Smith's *An Inquiry into the Nature and Causes of the Wealth of Nations* (Fife, 1776): "He intends only his own gain, and he is in this, as in many other cases, led by an invisible hand to promote an end which was no part of his intention."

Quarantine in the Borders
As the British government certified Northumberland the last of its regions free of Foot-and-Mouth disease, BBC World News 1/14/02 reported on American television that the number of animals slaughtered during 2001 totaled 4,000,000. Several months earlier they had reported the actual number of confirmed cases of the disease as 337. During the height of the crisis in spring 2001, *The Scotsman* reported that farmer suicides were averaging 1 per week.

'to ashes . . . to dust' / The Cattle of the Sun
This poem also responds to the 2001 epidemic and its aftermath,
an example perhaps of human numbers and overconsumption
leading to breakdown of systems, and draconian over-reaction in
or-der to curb disaster.
On Ash Wednesday, the first day of Lent, Christian communicants
receive a symbol of mortality in the form of ashes.
As a baby, the Greek god Hermes was a master thief and Apollo's
herds were his first rustle. The boy won forgiveness by inventing the
lyre from a tortoise's shell and presenting it to his uncle.

She Wanted My Hearts the Same Way
Written in honor of my living siblings, in memory of our dead, and
in memory of our parents.

Nemesis
Originally, this deity dispensed justice as the ruler of order, of
the procession of the seasons, of things done at the proper time,
adherence to the social rules. In later Greek mythology she
dispensed retribution and became associated with vengeance.

About to Burn Her Dress
In 1892, legendary Lizzie Borden (1860-1927) was tried and
acquitted, amidst much media publicity, for the axe murders of her
father and stepmother in Fall River, Massachusetts. She claimed to
have been in the barn at the time of their deaths.

Scottish Roots
Special thanks to Hawthornden Castle International Retreat for
Writers for this one.

Your Mouth on Me
Written in memory of Chuck Dockham.

Fresh Coffee After You Are Gone
Written in memory of my brother Tom.

Air
Especially, with love, for Peter Fortunato and our decades together.

ACKNOWLEDGMENTS

For the time and space that fostered many of these poems, I am deeply grateful to Hawthornden Castle and Macdowell. Indescribable gratitude to the Fine Arts Work Center for resetting my priorities.

Emaho! to Gary Snyder for the apprenticeship on San Juan Ridge.

Grateful acknowledgments are made to the editors of the following publications, in which some of these poems first appeared, sometimes in slightly different form: *AGNI, Chautauqua, Emily Dickinson Awards Anthology, Fourteen Hills, Hotel Amerika, LIT, Matter, Nimrod, Notre Dame Review, Passages North, Poetry, Seattle Review, Seneca Review, Shankpainter, Slant, Smartish Pace, Southern California Anthology, Stand, Stone Canoe, TAB, Tygerburning, Woven Tale Press,* and *Yellow Silk*

'About To Burn Her Dress' and 'The Woman In The Hat Paused, Mole-Eyed' appeared in *The Ruined Walled Castle Garden,* winner of the Bright Hill Press Poetry Chapbook Competition.

'About To Burn Her Dress,' 'God Of The Vine,' ' The Apprentice' [part 3 of Rosslyn Chapel's Artisans] were reprinted in *The Woven Tale Press.*

'Air' and 'Holy Island' are anthologized in *Wild Gods: The Ecstatic in Contemporary Poetry and Prose,* New Rivers Press.

'Leveled' won the Judith Siegel Pearson Award, Wayne State University, and was finalist for the Pablo Neruda Poetry Prize in the *Nimrod*/Hardman Awards.

'The Language of Bees' received a *BBC Wildlife Magazine* Poet of the Year Award.

'Quarantine in the Borders' is anthologized in *The &Now Awards: The Best Innovative Writing,* Lake Forest College Press.

'She Wanted My Hearts the Same Way' is anthologized in *Rumors Secrets & Lies,* Anhinga Press.

'We Live in Syn / Chronicity' won National Honorable Mention in the 9th annual Joe Gouveia Outermost Poetry Contest.

'Why She Can't Eat the Light' was awarded an Ann Stanford Prize.

ABOUT THE AUTHOR

Mary Gilliland is the author of two poetry collections: *Gathering Fire* and *The Ruined Walled Castle Garden*. Her work has been anthologized in *Nuclear Impact: Broken Atoms in Our Hands* and in *Wild Gods: The Ecstatic in Contemporary Poetry and Prose*. She is the recipient of a featured reading at the Al Jazeera International Film Festival, the Stanley Kunitz Fellowship at the Fine Arts Work Center in Provincetown, and a Council for the Arts Faculty Grant from Cornell University. She lives in Ithaca, New York, where she and her husband have transformed a rocky acre of the Six Mile Creek watershed into a woodland garden.